A HISTORY OF BRITAIN

Acknowledgments:

The author and publishers would like to thank Mike Gibson for his help in research, and the following for permission to use illustrative material:

Pages 18 and 19: The Institute of Agricultural History and Museum of Rural Life, University of Reading; 26 (bottom): R. Aitchison; cover and 23: Ashmolean Museum; 35 (top): the Marquis of Bath; 41: BBC Enterprises Ltd; 42: Phot. Bibl. Nat. Paris; 50: Britain on View; cover and 7 (top): the Trustees of the British Museum; 37: Pat Hodgson Library; 14, 20 (right), 27, 35 (centre and bottom): Michael Holford; 12, 31 (2): Hulton-Deutsch Collection; 33: Ipswich Museums and Galleries; 16/17, 26 (top and centre): Jarrold Colour Publications; cover (2) and 13, 30: A. F. Kersting; 17: drawing reference from King Edward VI School, Louth; 9, 24, 25, 32, 39, 44: The Mansell Collection; 45, 51 (2), 53: The Mary Rose Trust; 49 (top right): The Methuen Collection/ Corsham Court; 28: Museum of London; 14 (left): National Museums and Art Galleries of Merseyside/Walker Art Gallery, Liverpool; 43 (top left): National Museums of Scotland; 10 (top 3, bottom left, bottom right), 16, 21, 22: National Portrait Gallery, London; 47 (top left): National Trust Photographic Library; 43 (top right): His Grace the Duke of Norfolk and the Lady Herries; 10 (bottom centre): by gracious permission of Her Majesty the Queen; 15: Royal Armouries Board of Trustees; 38: The Shakespeare Birthplace Trust; 20 (left): Topham Picture Library; 47 (centre): Ulster Museum; 25, 36: the Victoria and Albert Museum; tapestry: Warwick Castle; 7 (centre), 49 (bottom left): the Dean and Chapter of Westminster Abbey.
Designed by Gavin Young.

Ladybird books are widely available, but in case of difficulty may be ordered by post or telephone from:

Ladybird Books – Cash Sales Department
Littlegate Road Paignton Devon TQ3 3BE
Telephone 0803 554761

A catalogue record for this book is available
from the British Library

Published by Ladybird Books Ltd Loughborough Leicestershire UK
Ladybird Books Inc Auburn Maine 04210 USA

Contents

The Tudors

by TIM WOOD
illustrations by PETER DENNIS

Series Consultants: School of History
University of Bristol

Ladybird

The Tudors

This book covers just over a hundred years, from the end of the Middle Ages to the start of the Stuart Period.

During this time, England, Wales, Scotland and Ireland, though not united, were all ruled by members of the powerful Tudor family. These years were peaceful compared with the violent times of the Middle Ages, although there were still problems, particularly over religion and the power of Parliament. For nearly half of this period, England was ruled by Elizabeth I, one of the best-loved English monarchs. By 1603, the English were united, proud of their country, and getting richer. The throne seemed safe at last.

Events during Tudor period

Date	Kings, Queens and People	Events
1450		Wars of the Roses
	Henry VII (1485-1509)	1485 battle of Bosworth

1500

Henry VIII
(1509-1547)
Cardinal Wolsey
Thomas Cromwell
Sir Thomas More

1534 Parliament declares
Henry head of the Church
of England
1536 Anne Boleyn executed
Closing of the monasteries
War with France and
Scotland

Edward VI
(1547-1553)

English prayer book
introduced

Mary I
(1553-1558)

Lady Jane Grey queen for
nine days
Persecution of Protestants
Alliance with Spain
1558 Loss of Calais

Elizabeth I
(1558-1603)
Lord Burleigh

Drake
Raleigh

Shakespeare

1600

Mary Queen of Scots flees
to England
Catholic plots against
Elizabeth
English ships attack
Spanish treasure ships
1587 Mary Queen of Scots
executed
1588 Armada defeated
War in Ireland
Poor Laws passed

5

A new age begins

Henry Tudor defeated King Richard III
at the battle of Bosworth Field in 1485.
When Richard was killed in the fight, his
crown was plucked from a bush and
placed on Henry's head. His death ended
the Wars of the Roses between the
Yorkists and Lancastrians, those members
of the royal family who had been
struggling for the throne for thirty years.

Henry VII crowned on the battlefield

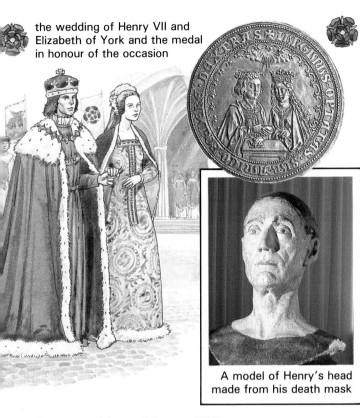

the wedding of Henry VII and Elizabeth of York and the medal in honour of the occasion

A model of Henry's head made from his death mask

The new king, Henry VII, was a Lancastrian. He made his claim to the throne stronger by marrying Elizabeth of York, his fourth cousin and a member of the opposite side, the Yorkists. Henry had lived abroad so the English people knew nothing of him and could never have imagined that his family was going to rule England for the next 120 years.

Henry VII

Henry brought peace to the country but he did not feel completely safe on his throne.

He believed that to be a strong king he needed to have plenty of money. He told his servants to collect as much money for him as they could. Then he made sure that he did not have to spend this money on wars because they were too expensive.

Henry checked the royal accounts every day to see how his money was being spent

Henry became a rich man. Although he was not a popular king, he was respected. When he died in 1509, he passed a safe and strong crown to his son, Henry VIII. When Henry VIII came to the throne however, he spent all his father's money fighting wars against France.

Henry had to put down two rebellions by men claiming his throne. One rebel, Lambert Simnel, was only thirteen years old. After beating his rebel army, Henry put Lambert to work in the royal kitchens. The other rebel, Perkin Warbeck, was trained by his tutor to pretend

Lambert Simnel

Perkin Warbeck

to be Richard, Duke of York, a member of the royal family. He was also captured but Henry had him executed.

Henry VIII and his wives

Two weeks after Henry VIII was crowned, he married Catherine of Aragon, a Spanish princess. Although she was a good wife to him, she did not give him a son. Henry thought that England would be weak if there were no king to follow him.

Catherine of Aragon
Had a daughter, Mary. Divorced

Anne Boleyn
Had a daughter, Elizabeth. Executed

Jane Seymour
Had a son, Edward. Died

Anne of Cleves
No children. Divorced

Catherine Howard
No children. Executed

Catherine Parr
No children. Outlived Henry

Henry asked the *Pope* to give him a divorce so that he could marry again. The Pope refused, so Henry broke away from the *Catholic* Church and set up his own Church of England. He divorced Catherine and married Anne Boleyn, a *lady-in-waiting*. Anne did not have a son either, and when Henry tired of her, he had her executed.

the execution of Anne Boleyn

His third wife Jane Seymour did give him a son, Edward, but she died twelve days later. Henry, becoming old and ill, married three more times.

Henry VIII and the monasteries

After he had made himself head of the new Church of England, Henry began to close the *monasteries*. Many monks had never accepted the new religion and Henry did not trust them because they still thought of the Pope as their leader.

Henry's chief minister, Thomas Cromwell, sent officials to investigate the monasteries

Cromwell

Henry, who was short of money, wanted the wealth of the monasteries for himself. Government officials reported that the monks were lazy and were not obeying the monastery rules. Henry used this as an excuse to close the monasteries and sell their land.

the ruins of Whitby Abbey

The monks were driven out and the monastery buildings were looted

Henry VIII's court

As a young king Henry was tall, handsome and intelligent. He was interested in music, books and sport. Eager to show off his wealth and power, he built several palaces, magnificently decorated with painted ceilings, and furnished with carpets and *tapestries*.

Henry VIII

Hampton Court Palace, the only one of Henry's palaces that has survived to this day. It was built by his minister, Cardinal Wolsey, and given by him to the king.

A game of blind man's buff

The king and his *courtiers* lived in the palaces. They dressed in their finest clothes and jewels. They were entertained with dancing, poetry readings and music. Outside, in the royal gardens and forests, all kinds of sport were played.

Henry's armour. He was a fine *jouster*, a good archer and a keen deer hunter

Edward VI, the boy king

When Henry VIII died in 1547, his only son Edward became king. Edward was just nine years old, so first his uncle, the Duke of Somerset, and then the Duke of Northumberland ruled England in his name.

Edward was never in good health and died at the age of fifteen.

Edward VI

King Edward VI Grammar School, Stratford-upon-Avon

Henry VIII had closed the monastery schools. During Edward's reign new grammar schools were started to teach boys to read and write. The most important subject taught was Latin.

Although letters were written in English, most important books were written in Latin. Hornbooks like this were used to teach pupils to read. There are only twenty four letters on this hornbook. At the time it was made, I was used to write I and J, and V was used to write both U and V

A B C D
E F G H
I K L M
N O P Q
R S T V
W X Y Z

Goosefeather *quills* were used for writing. Pupils had to sharpen the quills and mix their own ink

School teachers were very strict and beat their pupils with birches if they misbehaved

Changes in the countryside

By Tudor times, landowners had found that they could make more money by raising sheep for the wool trade than by growing corn to make bread. Since it was easier to look after sheep in an enclosed space, they began to plant hedges to make smaller fields. Soon much of the land, including the *commons*, had been enclosed.

a beehive

Many peasants kept bees. Honey was the only way the Tudors had of sweetening their food

Without the common land, the peasants could no longer grow enough food for themselves. Even worse, many of them lost their jobs because sheep did not need so many people to look after them.

The difficulties were even greater because the population had grown so fast that there was not enough bread to feed them.

Many peasants were so angry about the *enclosures* that they tore down the hedges, and demanded that land should be ploughed for corn.

a plough

In 1549, peasants in the Eastern counties rebelled, protesting about enclosures, high rents and low wages. Their leader Robert Ket and about fifty others were hanged.

Bloody Mary

Before Edward VI died, his ministers had persuaded him to make a will naming Lady Jane Grey as queen. They wanted her because although her claim to the throne was only slight, she was a *Protestant*. But Mary, Henry VIII's elder daughter, came to London to claim the throne. Lady Jane was arrested and later executed.

Mary had been an unhappy child. Her father, Henry VIII, divorced her mother, Catherine of Aragon, when Mary was

seventeen. Mary never forgave him. She was separated from her mother, ignored by her father and forgotten at court.

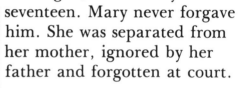

Mary married Philip II, the Catholic king of Spain. They had a strange marriage since they lived together for less than a year and had no children. The marriage made Mary very unpopular because it was feared that Spaniards would rule England.

Mary was a strong Catholic and when she became queen she was determined that England should return to the old religion. Nearly three hundred people who refused to give up the Protestant faith were burned at the stake.

Bishop Nicholas Ridley

Bishops Latimer and Ridley being burned at the stake in Oxford. It was believed that although the body was burned, the soul of the victim would go to Heaven.

A new Queen

young Queen Elizabeth

In 1558 Mary died and her sister Elizabeth became queen. The new queen faced many problems. She was short of money. England was threatened by Scotland, France and Spain. Elizabeth was a Protestant but she tried to make the Church of England acceptable to Catholics who were only charged a small fine if they did not go to the services.

Luckily Elizabeth was an intelligent, courageous and determined woman. She was also very popular with the people of England and became a much loved and respected ruler, known as Good Queen Bess.

Elizabeth's gloves. She was very proud of her long, slim fingers and loved fashionable clothes

The Elizabethan age began with Elizabeth's coronation. The crowds fought to cut little pieces off the blue carpet on which she walked, to keep as souvenirs

The royal progress

In August and September the court travelled around the south of England, staying in the houses of great *nobles*. A long procession of 400 carts and 2,400 packhorses carried the courtiers and their belongings.

Every time the procession came to a town the mayor and council would welcome the queen with speeches and gifts. Elizabeth travelled so that her people could see her and she could impress them.

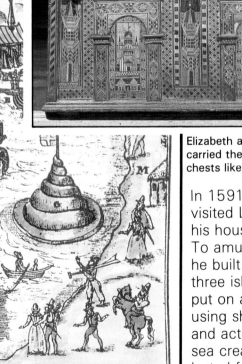

Elizabeth and her courtiers carried their possessions in chests like this one

In 1591, the court visited Lord Hertford at his house at Elvetham. To amuse the queen he built a lake with three islands in it. He put on a *pageant* using ships, musicians and actors dressed as sea creatures. The fun lasted for several days.

Tudor houses

Some people became very rich in Elizabeth's reign. They built houses like this one that were a lot more comfortable than medieval houses had been.

Many magnificent houses were built by rich nobles, often in the shape of an E. This is Condover Hall, Shropshire

Many houses were built with a timber frame filled in with plaster.

the Guildhall, Lavenham

Poor people lived in much smaller houses

Towns

The narrow streets of Tudor towns and cities were exciting, noisy places, crammed with people and carts. They were also very unhealthy. There was rubbish everywhere, and many people died of diseases spread by rats.

A London street in Tudor times (a model of Cheapside)

street trader

driving sheep
to market

flower
seller

water
seller

milk
maid

29

Beggars

During Elizabeth's reign there was a great increase in the number of poor people. This was partly because the population rose, but also because enclosures meant that there were fewer jobs so many people could not afford the high food prices. Many Elizabethans thought that people who were poor had only themselves to blame because they were simply lazy.

Poor people who were sick or old, and therefore thought to deserve help, could be looked after by their parish or given food at an almshouse like this one, Leycester's Hospital in Warwick.

In years when the harvest failed and food was short, people went hungry. They were forced to travel to look for food or charity. They were often joined by soldiers returning from wars abroad. Large groups of these beggars brought terror to whole towns as they attacked and robbed the townspeople. These beggars were punished in *houses of correction* by whipping or *branding* with hot irons.

Beggars were very skilful at making people feel sorry for them so that they would give more money. Some pretended to be horribly injured, others pretended to be mad

A soap eater. He ate soap to make himself froth at the mouth and pretended to have fits

Some beggars pretended to be mad

Crime and punishment

There was a lot of crime in Tudor times. There was no paid police force, so people had to look for the criminals themselves. Those who were caught were punished very harshly as an example to others. People could be hanged for stealing.

The gallows. Common people were hanged. Nobles were usually beheaded

Punishment for minor crimes

the stocks

whipping

The crimes of *treason*, rebellion, riot, murder and most kinds of stealing were all punished by death. Since modern police methods such as fingerprinting had not been invented, it was hard to prove a criminal was guilty so people were sometimes made to confess to crimes by torture.

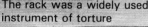
The rack was a widely used instrument of torture

a ducking stool

branding

pillory

Food

Rich Tudors ate a great deal of meat, except on one day each week when, by law, everyone had to eat fish instead. All meals, even those eaten by children, were washed down with wine or beer. They suffered from lots of diseases because their diet had few vitamins in it.

Breakfast 6am
Bean-porridge, Salted fish, Boiled Mutton, Bread.

Dinner 12 noon
Roast rib of beef, Roast leg of lamb, Rabbit pie, Pigeon stew, Peas, Bread, Butter, Cheese.

Supper 6pm
Leg of mutton stuffed with garlic, Venison pasty with sugared mustard, Boiled chicken with leeks, Roast blackbird, Pickled cabbage, Nuts, Cheese, Almond biscuits.

Poor people mainly ate vegetable stews and bread. Exciting but expensive new foods such as chocolate and chilli peppers were brought back from America.

A rich Tudor family eating

The Tudors suffered from bad teeth, partly because they did not drink enough milk, and partly because they ate too many sweet things. Queen Elizabeth had very black teeth.

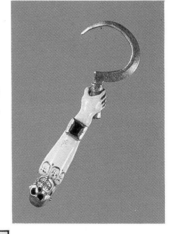

a toothpick
Sometimes a piece of linen was rubbed over the teeth as well

Tudor knives. Most people ate with their fingers, as forks were not widely used at the time

Sports and pastimes

Hunting for stags, deer and hares was very popular among landowners. Hunt picnics were arranged in the forests.

a virginal —
a type of early piano

The Elizabethans were very fond of dancing. In one dance, the volta, ladies jumped high in the air. Some people thought it disgraceful because the ladies showed their knees.

The Tudors were very fond of music

Printing had made books much cheaper. There were few story books but poetry was very popular

a lute – a sort of guitar

The theatre

The theatre was very popular in Elizabeth's reign. Religious plays which had been popular in the Middle Ages were banned, so new plays were written. These were performed in theatres, rather than, as they had been in the past, on wagons that travelled from town to town.

William Shakespeare. His plays are still performed all over the world and he is probably the most famous playwright who ever lived

In 1576, the first theatre was built in London so that actors could perform their plays on the same stage all year round. It was so successful that soon other theatres, like the *Fortune*, the *Swan* and the *Globe*, were built. In Tudor times, all the women's parts were played by boys. Often a bag of animal's blood was hidden under the actors' costumes to make stabbings and deaths look more real.

(below) The *Globe* theatre, where William Shakespeare once acted

What people wore

Tudor clothes changed a good deal from the time of Henry VII. The clothes of rich Elizabethans were much more splendid and extravagant, partly because Elizabeth herself was very interested in fashion.

gentleman during Henry VIII's reign

padded jacket called a doublet

lady during Henry VIII's reign

Ladies' headdresses were stiffened with wire and decorated with gold and jewels

velvet gown

woollen tights called hose tucked into the belt

Rich people often decorated their clothes with jewels. Some literally wore their entire fortunes on their backs.

woollen gown

Farmers' wives wore similar fashions but in much cheaper cloth

Makeup

This actress was made up to look like Elizabeth I for a TV series. The labels show what Elizabeth herself wore, much of which was very bad for her skin

plucked eyebrows

eyedrops made from Deadly Nightshade

cheeks coloured with red dye and egg-white

red wig

face painted with white lead and vinegar

rouge on lips

Starched collars called ruffs were supported by wire frames

neck ruff

very tight padded doublet

wrist ruffles

Skirts were supported by a wooden framework of hoops called a farthingale

Elizabethan ladies wore corsets stiffened with wood or iron

short cloak

Elizabethan men wore short padded trousers called breeches

Mary Queen of Scots

Mary Queen of Scots was a rival to Elizabeth. Mary was Elizabeth's cousin and would become queen if Elizabeth died without having any children. Mary fled to England to seek Elizabeth's protection after a rebellion of the Scottish lords in 1568.

Mary

Mary's jewels and fan, given to her by her servant, Giles Mowbray, just before her death

Mary's prayer book, and the *rosary* she used on the scaffold

Elizabeth signs
Mary's death warrant

Mary was also
a Catholic and many Catholics felt that
she should be queen instead of Elizabeth.
For nineteen years Mary was imprisoned
in various English castles.

Foolishly, she became involved in
Catholic plots against Elizabeth. When
proof of Mary's plotting was given to the
Queen, she sadly signed Mary's death
warrant.

Mary was executed at Fotheringhay
Castle in 1587.

Sea dogs

In 1492, Columbus discovered America for the King of Spain. The Spanish conquered the Aztecs and Incas who lived there, and took their land and wealth. Spanish treasure fleets, loaded with gold and silver, sailed across the Atlantic to land their cargoes in Spain. Spain became the richest country in Europe.

Sir Francis Drake. He became the first English sea captain to sail round the world. He attacked Spanish ports in America and stole over £1,500,000 of gold. The Spanish called him 'el draco' – the dragon.

FRANCISCVS DRACVS NOBILISS. EQVES ANGLIE

a Spanish galleon

Encouraged by Elizabeth, who wanted a share of the loot, English captains, nicknamed 'sea dogs', began to attack the slow Spanish galleons and steal the treasure they carried. To the Spanish king, Philip II, the sea dogs were little better than pirates. To the English, they became heroes.

The English ships were smaller but faster than the clumsy Spanish galleons. The sea dogs pounded the galleons with their cannon until they surrendered.

an English cannon called a culverin

The Armada

King Philip II of Spain grew more and more angry with Elizabeth because she encouraged her sea dogs to attack Spanish ships. She was also helping the Dutch Protestant rebels who were fighting against Spain.

Philip was a strong Catholic and he wanted England to be a Catholic country. He plotted to put Mary Queen of Scots on the throne of England but she was executed in 1587. The following year, Philip decided to take action and sent a great fleet, or armada, of 130 ships carrying 30,000 soldiers and sailors to invade England.

Beacon fires were lit across England to spread the news of the Armada's arrival

Treasure raised by divers from the wreck of an Armada ship

In spite of English attacks in the Channel, the Spanish fleet reached Calais safely. The English sent fireships into the Spanish fleet and it scattered in panic. A great storm blew up, driving the Spanish ships northwards. They had to sail right round Scotland. Many were wrecked and less than half of the Spanish ships managed to limp back to Spain. The Armada had failed.

The death of the Queen

On Thursday, 24th March 1603, a hush fell over London. Good Queen Bess had died, aged nearly seventy. Elizabeth had never married, and she had no children to follow her. She was the last Tudor ruler.

Elizabeth's funeral

Few of her subjects remembered what it was like to be ruled by a king. She had shown that a woman could rule as well as any man. Though she had become less popular in later years, her reign had been one of the most glorious in English history.

Elizabeth in old age

As soon as Elizabeth died, a messenger galloped north to tell King James VI of Scotland, the son of Mary Queen of Scots, that he was to be crowned James I of England. He was the first of a new family of rulers – the Stuarts.

Elizabeth's tomb in Westminster Abbey

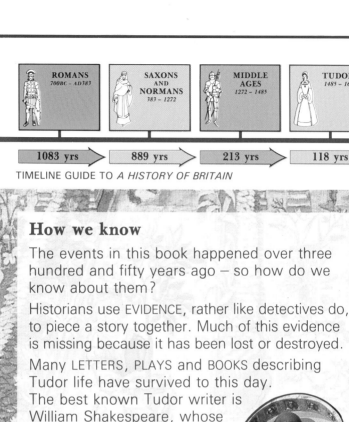

| ROMANS 700BC – AD383 | SAXONS AND NORMANS 383 – 1272 | MIDDLE AGES 1272 – 1485 | TUDORS 1485 – 1603 |

| 1083 yrs > | 889 yrs > | 213 yrs > | 118 yrs > |

TIMELINE GUIDE TO *A HISTORY OF BRITAIN*

How we know

The events in this book happened over three hundred and fifty years ago – so how do we know about them?

Historians use EVIDENCE, rather like detectives do, to piece a story together. Much of this evidence is missing because it has been lost or destroyed.

Many LETTERS, PLAYS and BOOKS describing Tudor life have survived to this day. The best known Tudor writer is William Shakespeare, whose plays give interesting pictures of Tudor life.

William Shakespeare

Among the letters which have survived are the love letters Henry VIII wrote to Anne Boleyn. All sorts of papers were kept by the government and landowners, and while the handwriting is hard to read, they help us to understand how Tudor people lived.

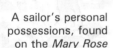

A sailor's personal possessions, found on the *Mary Rose*

There are still a lot of BUILDINGS that have survived to this day. There is a list of places to visit on page 56.

Archaeologists have excavated many Tudor sites. One of the most interesting is the wreck of a Tudor ship called the *Mary Rose*. This was like a time capsule which contained thousands of objects all from the same period.

OBJECTS found by archaeologists are often stored in museums. There is a list of museums to visit on page 56.

Some of these old objects seem strange to us. What do you think these are? They were found in the wreck of the *Mary Rose*. You will find the answer on page 56

The legacy of the Tudors

At the start of the Tudor period most people thought the world was flat. Few sailors had travelled far from the coast, so Europeans had no idea what the world really looked like.

By the end of the period, explorers had sailed across the Atlantic and found the vast continents of the Americas. Sea captains, like Sir Francis Drake and Thomas Cavendish, sailed right round the world and so started a new age of travel, trade and settlement.

Cocoa, pineapples and turkeys were all found by Christopher Columbus in the West Indies in 1492. They reached England a few years later

Tobacco and potatoes were discovered by Sir Walter Raleigh on his trip to America in 1585. When Raleigh smoked his first pipeful of tobacco, his servant thought he was on fire and threw a pot of ale over him!

Several mathematical symbols were first used in Tudor times. Among them were the + sign, the − sign and the = sign

Rockets and hand grenades were first used in war in Tudor times

Chimneys were first used in Tudor times, making fires much more efficient and putting an end to smoke-filled rooms. As a result, houses became much more comfortable, with many more rooms, each with its own fireplace

In 1570 a Spanish nobleman invented the first toothbrush

Astronomers said that the old idea that the sun went round the Earth was wrong. They claimed that actually the Earth went round the sun. However, few people believed them!

Near the end of the period the first screw appeared. It was really a nail with a thread on it. It was hammered in, but could not be removed until the invention of the screwdriver more than a hundred years later!

The first pencil was made in 1565 in Switzerland. Its lead was made of pure graphite, and its cover was wood. Modern pencil leads are made of graphite and clay

The first pocket watch was made in 1500 in Germany.
Sailors sometimes had pocket sundials like this one found on the *Mary Rose*

Glossary

branding: burning with a red-hot iron

Catholic: see Roman Catholic

common: land on which peasants had the right to graze their animals

courtier: a person at the royal court

enclosure: dividing the land and surrounding the new fields with hedges

house of correction: where poor people were given food in exchange for work, and were also punished when necessary

jousters: men who fought on horseback with lances

lady-in-waiting: one of the queen's attendants

monastery: a house where monks live and work

noble: a person of high rank such as a lord

pageant: an entertainment based on historic events and people

Pope: the head of the Roman Catholic Church

Protestant: a Christian not of the Catholic Church

Roman Catholic: a member of the Church of Rome

rosary: a string of beads used while saying prayers

quill: a pen made from a sharpened bird's feather

tapestry: a picture woven in cloth

treason: treachery against your own country

Index

Places to visit

HOUSES, CASTLES and PALACES

Adlington Hall, Cheshire
Anne Hathaway's Cottage, Stratford-upon-Avon
Arreton Manor, Isle of Wight
Arundel Castle, West Sussex
Berkeley Castle, Gloucestershire
Bramhall Hall, Greater Manchester
Broughton Castle, Oxfordshire
Buckland Abbey, Devon
Burghley House, Cambridgeshire
Hampton Court Palace, London
Hardwick Hall, Derbyshire
Hever Castle, Kent
Holyrood Palace, Edinburgh
Kenilworth Castle, Warwickshire
Knole, Kent
Little Moreton Hall, Cheshire
Longleat, Wiltshire
Montecute House, Somerset
Penshurst Place, Kent
Speke Hall, Merseyside
Temple Newsam House, Leeds
Warwick Castle, Warwickshire
West Stow Hall, Sussex
Woburn Abbey, Bedfordshire
Wollaton Hall, Nottinghamshire

MUSEUMS

British Museum, London
City Museum, Plymouth
Elizabethan House, Plymouth
London Museum
Merchant's House, Plymouth
Tower of London

Answer to objects on page 51: The objects are arrow
holders for storing arrows. The holes held the arrows apart
so that their feather flights would not touch.